Talkshō

Talkshō

Haiku & Senryu
by Stephen Koritta

SNARK PUBLISHING
O'Fallon, Illinois

This publication was funded by:

Snark Publishing Foundation
637 West Highway 50 #119
O'Fallon, IL 62265
        www.snarkpub.com

Author Contact: HonestJak@aol.com

ISBN 0-9728948-0-2
Printed in the United States of America

5 4 3 2 1

To my parents
who have encircled me
with hope.

Contents

Acknowledgements ix

Spring 1

Summer 9

Autumn 17

Winter 25

Neighborhood Watch 31

Weekend Condition 53

About the Author 69

Illustrations

1   Pond at Seiwa-En

9   Infernal

17   Purple Geese

25   Glacial

31   Dusk House (detail)

35   Rooftop Ghost (detail)

40   Skyline

48   Flora

53   Blue Self

57   Hither Glance

61   Departure from Stone

66   Gesso Dove

Cover design and all illustrations
are by the author.

Acknowledgements

The realization of this collection in print was substantially due to the faith and generosity of P F Allen and Steve Heffern of Snark Publishing.

I am grateful as well for the kind words and encouragement of Donna Biffar, Wayne Lanter, and Phillip Miller, the editors of River King Poetry Supplement.

The friendship of Greg Levrault, Jason Akley, Fred Clark, Sheri Allen, Sharon Cox, and Bryan Rickert has sustained me throughout.

Spring

Déjà vu of vase
as it recalls having held
this first flower.

Distracting tapping –
A downy probes the doorpost
for a grub.

Rufouses roughhouse,
their wings
invisibly busy.

Beneath the birdbath,
the ousted housecats crouch
waist-deep in daisies.

In the mouth
of the cat-shaped topiary,
a sparrow's nest.

Where the pruning shears
have come unclenched from branch,
the shoots resume.

Spreading as ever
over the flowered couch,
catalogues of seed.

Jargon of the garden –
Even humble bramble plants
have Latin roots.

Toad takes a load off.
The lake, a lazy paisley
of lily pads.

Prairie grass...cattail –
Dragonflies agonize
over where to land.

A thousand mouths –
Gaping carp nip at the heels
of yesterday's bread.

Sprays of coins and koi
spatter the water bottom
with a copper pox.

Hyde Park in March –
Inchworms on the bench's arm
convert to metric.

Lurking worker bee –
Yellow lapel pin
mistook for a stamen.

How many dawns?
On every stem, an abacus
of dew beads.

Night sky and wheat field –
Crop of stars, harvested
by gathering clouds.

Basho,
shadowed by banana tree,
waiting out the rain.

Nimbus does its business –
One wet shingle hangs
over low eaves.

Newspaper, slipper,
big dipper and bug zapper –
Front porch fortunate.

Book has blown open…
Again, the wind picks up
where it left off.

Summer

June sun, newly up –
A ripened rose reopens
for bee-business.

Summer again!
Patterns of wrought iron bench-backs
copied to soft skin.

Gob of ice in the waterglass
comes unstuck mid-sip.
My chin is drenched.

Glimpsing a tanned face
in the tent sale vanity –
Both of us browsing.

Sound of vows,
din of instamatic advance –
Red-eyed bride is flash-blind.

Pair of rhinestone stars
in pierced ears begin to burn –
She's been talked about.

Someone's spent stick of blackjack,
chewed by shoe bottoms
on the stone footpath.

Abandoned ranch house –
Ropes of over-ripe grapes
lassoed the gate shut.

Summer Garden –
Skin of the onion underwritten
by rot.

Almost August –
Still, a bottle rocket stick
reddens the dead grass.

Behind a coin laundry,
scent of summer dumpsters
stuffed with dryer sheets.

Same joy-cries that came
from the coaster's first row,
reenacted in back.

Summer thunderstorm –
The batting cages damaged
by baseball-sized hail.

A thirsty wasp,
inches his way down the rain gage –
Ground already dry.

Dusty, August lawn –
The gazing ball is polished
with a fish-eye sleeve.

Abnormally firm –
Forearms of the farmgirls,
housed in a hose-spray haze.

No two nights the same.
Coordinates of gnats
on the door-screen.

Ball jar by the bed –
Strobing beams of firefly light
through a holey lid.

A roaring fire –
Wishing to squish the insect,
tired hikers clap.

Restless housefly,
roosting on the Tao Te Ching
and then the crucifix.

Light, almost gone –
Books I'd not yet finished
footnoted by yawns.

Autumn

Each "Lost dog" leaflet
has fallen from its phone pole.
It must be Autumn.

Sulfury smells
lilt from the smelting mill –
This jaundiced dawn.

Newly loose
from the mooring of morning,
the little, leaf skiff.

Walking and cawing,
a weird iridescent wet
of lacquered blackbird.

Searching back and forth,
chickadee perched on the stick
where his feeder was.

A pair of sparrows,
feasting on the pampas top,
ride its droop to earth.

Mock orange –
One hundred trunks,
one tree.

Leaf caught on cobweb.
One twig balanced on its end –
Autumn mobile.

Treacherous nature trail –
A walking stick walking
on my walking stick.

Fate of the aphid
too bleak to think about,
his leaf on the fire.

Spark that leapt from leaf,
to shrub, to tree,
drains the hydrant dry.

On the courthouse steps,
murder of crows is reduced
to a lesser charge.

Mini-golf engulfed
and soaked are the go-cart tracks –
Branson abandoned.

Tackles of cattle
huddle in wind-blown end zones
of a thistle field.

Bits of dead box elder
bedapple the saplings
of the forest floor.

The ring and rattle
of ladder against gutter –
Downspout spits its leaves.

The wind is endless.
Wrists with hypodermic pricks
of painful rainfall.

Mixed with squeaks of gate,
the horned owl
has rephrased his question.

Gardener leaps, then laughs.
Raked from this year's underbrush,
last year's plastic snake.

At the back porch step,
a Frisbee fills with drizzle.
The wet dachshund drinks.

Late October –
Jostled nostrils of the jogger
with a winter tint.

Winter

Snow on the porch,
dust on the shelftops –
Only my throat clears.

Shivers
as overshoes nudge the muddy news
from under a thorn bush.

Utility line –
All thirteen of its blackbirds
look one way.

Early snow –
We see the slithery history
of a garden hose.

Sled must be buried.
Flat roof on the woodshed
announces inches.

Unplowed lots at the middle school
"O"ed
with snow-day doughnuts.

November window –
Collected works of frost
published on the panes.

Snowy road –
How many miles 'til Chicago?
Highway sign, bleached speechless.

Empty can of antifreeze –
Some poor, roadside sod
does the stranded dance.

Hunters in the snow
retrace asymmetric tracks
of limping hounds.

Mucussed acoustics
of a winter church –
The coughers are full.

Throat, just short of sore –
A warm, December bender
of toddy heat.

Cold studio –
A pimply Olympia
shivers from her pose.

Stone swan on a stand
in a statuary niche,
molting melted snow.

One week until spring –
Bouquets of crazed crows
on the privet bush.

Neighborhood Watch

Day about to break –
Cricket, toad and locust
empty their tip jars.

Up from pleasing sleep,
shapes of dawn
stray through drawn drapes.

Bed in the making,
frustrates the fraying stuff
that fills the pillow.

Freshly fitted sheet –
Geriatric tabby cat
kittenized in sleep.

Countertop, two cups –
Kettle still too cold
to steep the tea.

In the skillet,
the melted butter pat –
Egg has yet to crack.

After six breakfasts,
artifact at the box bottom
has been unearthed.

With every wind-shift,
cardboard yard sale arrows
face a different way.

Buried under sweats,
weights on the bar burden none
but the lifting bench.

Nostalgic wall clock –
it's cat eyes look left, right,
then left again.

Folding retriever,
poker face of the pug dog –
Bassett has a straight.

One matched set
of broken badminton rackets –
Roof is rife with cocks.

The young unmarried –
Her ringless hand weighs carrots
on a grocer's scale.

In a vinegar bath,
umbilicals of dill pickles
still attached.

Row of grocery lanes –
Barcode scanners banter
in tuneless unison.

From market to car,
egg dozen nestled to her breast.
Child rides the cart.

Eight flights of stairs –
Heavy breathing abbreviating
her swear words.

Noon,
Glass not yet washed –
Curdled circle of morning milk.

Lunch hour –
anxious grace-sayer looks both ways
before crossing himself.

Tops lopped off by haze –
High-rise buildings balding
in the stainless still.

Only one floor up,
the elevator loiters.
Buttons touched by ghosts.

40

Odor of toner –
Sung asleep by paper quires
in the copy room.

Among the clutter,
old solar calculator.
Equal sign worn off.

4:59 –
We are shown the verso side
of the "open" sign.

Shop has just locked up –
Sound of "shave-and-a-haircut"
on the barber's door.

Stopped by the slow freight.
Now, two towns down the line,
stopped by it again.

Small mill town –
Hearse and ambulance fill
at the same station.

Making clay ruts,
farm implement limping
down a rural route.

Pinball machine,
strapped to a flatbed's back,
tilting in the turns.

Used car lot –
not once do the cat's paws
touch asphalt.

Having no nest,
bird on the old Ford's hood
begins to rust.

Decapitated by bat,
mailbox flies its flag
at half staff.

If not for flailing tails,
cats on the attic sills
could be still lifes.

Dogs tied in side yards,
likable by bicycle
but not on foot.

Up the slide ladder,
five only-children
become quintuplets.

At opposite ends,
talkative kids pitch their chat
across the pond.

Line drives past the porch
have foreshadowed the shatter
of storm door glass.

Latchkeys in khakis
have suckled their dreamsickles.
Street, now humorless.

Arithmetic book shuts at dusk.
Boy is weary
from carrying ones.

Watching the pot do
what a watched pot never does –
Cupful of rice.

On the window screen,
we have seen the meal prayers
of a famished mantis.

Steam from the rump roast –
Family of four digresses
from grace to game scores.

48

Just hatched from its pan,
a bundt cake,
circumferenced with crumbs.

Empty dinner table –
Posthumous plumes tangle
above snuffed candles.

Finding a lost "I"
between the sofa cushions –
Double-word score!

Light goes on...
Two spatting attic spiders scatter
to neutral corners.

Second coat of paint –
Off-white hints of gone pictures
ghost the old nails.

Hendrix record skips –
A cherished air guitar
returns to its case.

Room, lit by reruns –
Color of her pullover
has faded to couch.

Contract on the desk –
Sunset, lamp and candle flame
shine in triplicate.

Shallow bowl –
Betta fish, surfacing for air,
kisses his reflection.

Wall shadowed with dad
as he nods through *The Shadow*...
Radio signs off.

Weekend Condition

Lovebirds and buzzards
flock for cups of coffee –
Late show just let out.

Clearly, she hears me.
Her head nods, serenaded
by "Mmm hmmm." hums.

In prolonged ping-pongings
of easygoing gazing,
she ties the game.

Raked into piles
of receipts seeped in grease,
greenery of tip.

Lines, thin as the tracks
made by snakes after sandstorms,
her frail profile.

Skinny people necking,
make a beast
with one-and-a-half backs.

She gives goodbye vibes,
euthanizing the night
while it's still young.

Carsick...sarcastic,
two plastered passengers ask
where I get off.

Empty Guinness glass –
Reel on the Uilleann pipe
has rolled to a stop.

Tattered adverts
of long-since-broken rock bands –
Boarded up nightclub.

Open mic. night notes
bouncing off the alley walls –
Whiff of distant joints.

High-dollar bar –
Even the player piano
has a tip jar.

Some standing, some dancing,
legs
of the Degas painting.

Titillating light –
Beneath the mirrored ball,
a plague of low-cuts.

When one is drunk,
even the skirted girl on the restroom sign
looks good.

Above the flush valve,
sixty-seven expletives
and a heart.

From the bandstand –
the thundery one…two…three
of mic. check.

As the lutes tune,
a skittish pizzicato.
The tension builds.

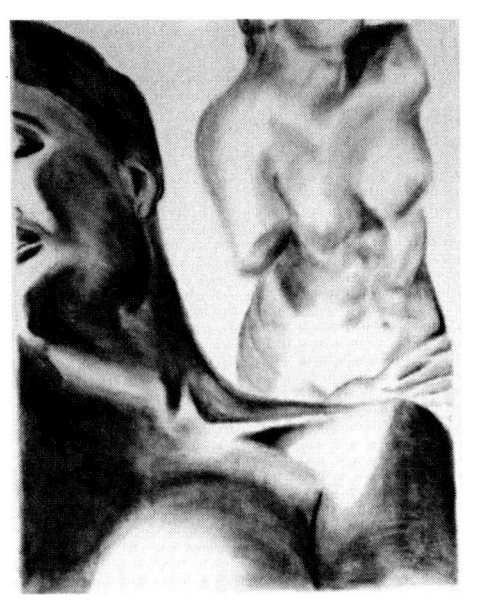

For lack of backbone,
a baritone saxophone
supports a sports shirt.

Several semi-quavers late,
one muted trumpet lisps
in lieu of flutes.

Swaying cheek-to-cheek
to moonlight Sinatra –
Hand strays from back to waist.

He calls for ballads
but gets blues –
Mutiny on the downbeat.

By the bridal suite,
maid said she turned down the bed…
but I still hear it.

Return trip –
Fog of windows fended off
with a stolen towel.

Head-lit hints
of bent fence, branch or antler...
soon, we will know which.

Faded "For sale" signs –
Fifty-seven Chevys
orphaned at road forks.

Pulling into Louisville –
Kentucky Rain
on the radio.

Rock-piles rise like breasts
before a bare driveway.
I've been alone too long.

Lewd pseudonyms on signs
outside the gentleman's club,
dimmed at daybreak.

Flavor of rain
and pain reliever,
the headache's hex.

Just in from a gig,
singer slings his smoky coat
over the armchair.

Jazz musician passes,
his whole life flashing
before his ears.

Above the town,
noon tones of bells from five spires
theologize.

About the Author

Stephen Koritta is a graduate of Belleville Area College with an Associate of Arts degree.

His poems have appeared in *River King Poetry Supplement*, *Intermission*, and *The Moon Reader*.

He is a winner of the 2001 *Metrolines*, a contest held annually by Arts in Transit and the International Writers Center at Washington University.

He is an active board member of the Saint Louis Poetry Center.

An accomplished musician and lyricist, Koritta provided bass, guitar and backing harmonies to Fred Clark's *Living in Dakin's Neighborhood* album. He has also contributed lead vocals and lyrics to Jon Thomas' *Green With Passion* release.